**CHRIS &
MATHILD
STUART**

C000003834

Avian
architects

Quick ID guide to nests and eggs
of southern African birds

Published by Struik Nature
(an imprint of Penguin Random House
South Africa (Pty) Ltd)
Reg. No. 1953/000441/07
The Estuaries No. 4, Oxbow Crescent,
Century Avenue, Century City, 7441
PO Box 1144, Cape Town, 8000 South Africa

Visit www.penguinrandomhouse.co.za and
join the Struik Nature Club for updates, news,
events and special offers.

www.stuartonnature.com

First published in 2021
10 9 8 7 6 5 4 3 2 1

ISBN 978 177584 743 4 (Print)
ISBN 978 177584 744 1 (ePub)

Copyright © in text, 2021: Chris &
    Mathilde Stuart
Copyright © in photographs and illustrations,
    2021: Chris & Mathilde Stuart, unless
    otherwise indicated alongside images
Copyright © in published edition, 2021:
    Penguin Random House South Africa
    (Pty) Ltd

Publisher: Pippa Parker
Managing editor: Roelien Theron
Designer: Gillian Black
Proofreader: Thea Grobbelaar

Reproduction by Studio Repro
Printed and bound by Novus Print, South Africa

Front cover Top: Village Weaver; Main
image: Green-backed Heron (John Carlyon);
Eggs (left to right): Bokmakierie, Red-
knobbed Coot, Verreaux's Eagle; Little
Grebe on nest (John Carlyon); Sociable
Weaver nest
Half-title page Top: Cape Weaver; Main
image: Sociable Weaver nest in quiver tree
Back cover Bottom left to right: Black-
headed Oriole (Penny Meakin), Black-
collared Barbet (John Carlyon)

Acknowledgements:
We thank Ernest Pringle
for allowing us access to
the bird egg collection
of his late father (Victor
Pringle) and Dave Allen
for granting us permission
to use the Durban Natural
Science Museum's
comprehensive bird egg
collection. Thanks also to
John Carlyon and Penny
Meakin, as well as the late
Alan Weaving, for use of
their images.

Note: All bird eggs
in this guide were
photographed in
long-established
private or museum
collections.

Contents

Introduction

Birds' nests come in an astonishing array of shapes and sizes. The first nests were most likely simple scrapes on the ground. Today stone curlews, terns, plovers, lapwings and the ostrich all lay and incubate their eggs in this type of nest. The next step was to make the nest more homely by adding bits of material around the eggs. Then a few species moved their nests off the ground, into bushes and trees, possibly as protection from predators. These first 'true' nests were probably simple and flimsy stick platforms, similar to those built by pigeons and doves today.

A pair of Grey Herons work together to build their large platform-style nest.

The cup nest emerged next – an evolutionary miracle with protective side 'walls' and a soft inner lining that provides more protection for eggs and chicks and, importantly, better insulation to aid incubation. The passerines build this type of open nest, while warblers and several of the larks have added other features, such as a domed roof, to conceal their eggs and nestlings from predators. Some species, like the weavers, have gone 'big', creating large, enclosed masterpieces using only their beaks as construction tools.

Other birds prefer taking up residence in existing cavities in trees, the ground or earth banks. Such a strategy conserves energy, and keeps nesting birds and their broods safe. Some kingfishers, the wood-hoopoes, rollers, hornbills and parrots make use of natural cavities, while barbets and woodpeckers excavate their own holes in trees, and bee-eaters and some kingfishers in earth banks.

This short guide is an introduction to the wonder of birds' nests and eggs. The numbered photographs show a variety of nest designs, eggs and birds. These are paired with the text to help you identify the nest types and the species that built them. Photographs of the eggs show colour and pattern variations where they occur. In addition, the average length of the eggs is given. Always keep a safe distance at nesting sites and take care not to disturb the birds, their eggs, or their chicks. The disturbance or collection of birds' eggs and nests is illegal.

Giant tree nests: Domed giants

The nest of the **Hamerkop (1)** is an extraordinary creation. A complex domed structure, it may weigh 50kg and reach up to 2m in height and width – quite a feat for a bird that tips the scales at less than 500g. The nest is usually constructed in the fork of a tree **(2&3)**, or sometimes on a cliff ledge **(4)**. It is made of twigs, reeds, grass and animal bones, and includes a mud-lined tunnel that leads to a chamber up to 50cm in diameter. A clutch of 1–5 eggs **(5)**, 46mm long, is laid. Nests near urban areas often include human waste such as plastic, rope and even toys. Years ago, the authors lived in the grounds of a mission hospital where the nest of the resident

Hamerkops featured discarded drip sets, soiled bandages and even syringes. This observation resulted in a revamp of the hospital's waste disposal policy!

Despite their small size, **Sociable Weavers** (<32g) **(6)** build colossal nests, more than 7m wide and capacious enough to house a colony of a few hundred birds. These domed communal nests are usually constructed in trees **(7)**, on telegraph poles or on the towers of windmills **(8)**. The nest's domed roof is made from twigs and may be embellished with thorns and coarse grasses, while the belly, or understorey, is crafted from finer grasses. Inside, individual nest chambers are occupied by a pair of birds, and are linked to the outside by a 25cm-long tunnel. Usually 3–4 eggs **(9)**, 21mm in length, are laid. Several other species of bird have been found roosting and nesting in the nest chambers of these large structures – one of which is the **Pygmy Falcon (10)**. Its white faeces **(11)** reveals the bird's presence.

Verreaux's Eagles (1) make some of the largest cliff nests **(2&3)**. These nests are expanded with each breeding season, and some structures can reach an impressive 4m in height and more than 1.5m in diameter. The nest bowl **(4)** is lined with green leaves, which are diligently replenished throughout the egg and nestling period. Two eggs, measuring 75mm in length, are laid at a time, but on hatching the older chick always kills the younger. The eggs **(5a&b)** may vary in coloration and pattern. Over time, the area below the nest becomes littered with the skulls of hyrax (dassies), the main prey of these eagles.

The **White-necked Raven (6)** builds its large bowl nest of sticks **(7)** on a cliff ledge, usually in extremely hard-to-reach locations. The fairly deep bowl is well lined with grass, hair and sheep's wool **(8)**. Wool soiled by nestlings is removed and replaced with fresh supplies; the discarded material is usually left in bushes nearby **(9)**. When nestlings are present, the area around the nest may become littered with broken tortoise carapaces and other food items (as the authors observed in the Karoo). Usually 4–5 eggs **(10a&b)**, measuring 50mm, are laid. Eggs may vary in coloration and pattern.

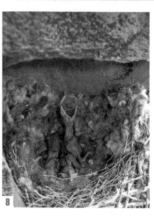

The nests of **swallows** and some of their close relatives are true marvels of construction. These nests are built with hundreds – and in some cases thousands – of individual mud pellets **(1)**, all of which the swallows collect and mould into place using their small, delicate bills.

Some birds, such as the **Lesser Striped Swallow (2)** and **Greater Striped Swallow (3)**, build a closed bowl with a long tubular entrance **(4)** – variations include nests with an unusually long entrance **(5)** or constructed from different mud sources **(6)**.

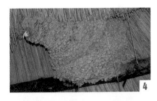

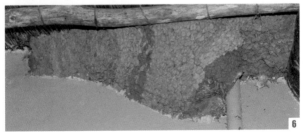

The **Rock Martin (7)** creates a simple half-cup nest, similar to the nest **(8)** of its kin, the Pearl-breasted Swallow.

The **South African Cliff Swallow's** nest **(9&10)** is a variation on the closed-bowl design: the entrance,

which is to the side near the top of the structure, is not always elongated into a tube. These swallows commonly construct their nests in colonies under bridges and in culverts, or on cliffs, with the nests crowded together and the nest walls touching each other. Nests are sometimes colonised for roosting by White-rumped Swifts, Cape Sparrows and occasionally Acacia Pied Barbets.

A Greater Striped
   Swallow:
   22mm
B Lesser Striped
   Swallow:
   20mm
C South African
   Cliff Swallow:
   20mm
D Rock Martin:
   21mm

Woven nests: Master weavers

Weavers are the avian world's master builders. Some, such as the **White-browed Sparrow-Weaver (1–3)** and the **Red-headed Weaver (4–6)**, construct rather messy but nevertheless impressive homes, whereas true weavers braid intricate ball nests with fine strips of green grass, shredded palm fronds and other material.

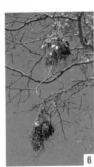

Imagine being told to build your new home using only your mouth – a seemingly impossible task. Yet that is exactly what a weaver male does, creating not only one but several nests until one of them meets with his mate's approval. The homes of species such as the **Spectacled (7)** and **Dark-backed weavers (8)** are embellished with long entrance tunnels. Like most weavers, the **Village Weaver (9)** and **Southern (10)** and **Lesser (11&12) masked weavers** build kidney-shaped lodgings, with the entrance beneath and to the side to prevent the eggs from falling out, especially in strong winds.

The home of the **Chestnut Weaver (13)** is sturdy but more untidy than that of other weavers. The **Cape Weaver male (14)** creates a relatively large nest **(15)**, with the female preferring the design of her new abode to include a short, fairly narrow entrance tunnel. The home of the **Eastern Golden Weaver (16)** also has a short tunnel, while the nests of the **Yellow Weaver (17)** and **Southern Brown-throated Weaver** lack this feature altogether. The roosting nest of the **Thick-billed Weaver (18)** has a larger entrance hole **(19)** than its breeding nest.

Most weavers nest in colonies – in reedbeds **(20)**, drooping branches of trees, palm fronds and even on telephone poles. The colonies of some species can comprise up to 300 breeding males.

A **Southern Masked Weaver** (4 clutches): 22mm
B **Dark-backed Weaver**: 23mm
C **Spectacled Weaver** (2 clutches): 22mm
D **Lesser Masked Weaver**: 21mm
E **Cape Weaver**: 25mm
F **Thick-billed Weaver** (2 clutches): 24mm
G **White-browed Sparrow-Weaver**: 25mm

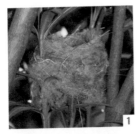

The classic open, cup-shaped nest, ranging from large and bulky to small and delicate, is the nest we most commonly associate with birds. There are several advantages to this design: they can protect and conceal eggs and chicks more effectively than simple platform structures, and they allow for better temperature control measures.

Although nest material varies according to species, most cup nests are constructed from course items such as twigs, bark or sticks, while the interior is lined with fine, soft components including leaves and grasses. The nests are usually well hidden – normally on the ground or in underground burrows, trees and tree hollows, and dense bush. Some birds, such as the **African Reed Warbler**, weave nests **(1)** that are attached to the stems of reeds. The rather bulky nests of the **Bokmakierie (2)** and **Kalahari Scrub Robin (3)** are located in shrubs or thorny bush, where they are difficult to see.

Nests built in exposed locations are often well camouflaged, making it difficult for predators to spot them. The **African Paradise Flycatcher (4)** constructs a delicate framework of very fine twigs or bark bound together with the silken threads of spiderwebs. The exterior walls are usually exquisitely camouflaged with lichen. The tiny cup nests of White-

John Carlyon

eyes, including **Cape White-eyes (5)**, are made of plant and animal fibres, woven together with spider webbing and suspended from a secluded horizontal branch. The construction materials serve as camouflage to conceal the nest from predators.

John Carlyon

The home **(6)** of the **Cape Bunting** is typically a rather untidy collection of grass, roots and twigs that is made more habitable by a soft, neat lining on the inside. Cape Buntings usually nest in bushes in rocky or hilly terrain. In the central Karoo their nests are nearly always located next to the base of a rock.

Mountain Wheatears (7) build substantial nests. The base is an amalgam of twigs, pieces of earth, stones and coarse grass, and the inside of the cup is luxuriously decked with sheep's wool, fine grass and other soft plant material.

The **Red-winged Starling's** home **(8)** is often built on a foundation of mud topped with a hefty mass of plant matter; the interior walls are covered with finer plant fibres. These birds construct their nests on cliff ledges, in caves or in buildings.

A **African Reed Warbler:** 18mm

B **Bokmakierie:** 26mm

C **Familiar Chat:** 20mm

D **Red-winged Starling:** 34mm

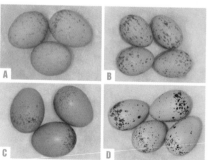

Penny Meakin

A number of birds have taken the simple cup nest to new, elaborate heights. Designs include the hammock-like nest of the **Black-headed Oriole (1)**, with its deep cup crafted from lichen, moss, grasses and spider silk, and the purse-like hanging nest of the **Long-billed Crombec (2)**, a digs made resplendent with cobwebs and fluffy seed 'wool'.

But the award for the most fascinating nest in the African avian world must go to the **Cape Penduline Tit**. Its oval, domed bag **(3)** of tightly felted woolly animal and plant fibres features a tubular entrance near the top, which is closed by the bird once inside the nest. Below the entrance is a ledge on which the bird can perch while using its foot to open the entrance from the outside. The nest of the **Grey Penduline Tit (4)** is generally smaller than that of its relative. Apart from providing a secure home for eggs and chicks, the nest serves as a roost for adults during and outside the breeding season.

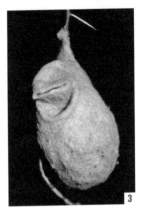

John Carlyon

L Tranter

The **Little Swift (5)** crafts its architectural wonder largely out of feathers and dry grass **(6&7)**, glued together with saliva. The end result is a closed bowl with a small side-top entrance. Several nests may adjoin each other, and are commonly built under eaves, bridges and rock overhangs. These swifts are highly colonial and when breeding they fly around in tightly packed 'screaming mobs'.

A **Black-headed Oriole:** 29mm
B **Long-billed Crombec:** 19mm
C **Cape Penduline Tit:** 14mm
D **Little Swift:** 23mm

K.Stuart

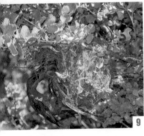

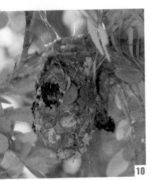

Sunbirds construct small, oval nests, usually from fine plant material, lichens and considerable quantities of spider silk, with a side entrance near the top. Some species build a simple entrance for their nests, while others, such as the **Greater Double-collared Sunbird (8)**, construct a sheltered porch over the entrance. The **Malachite Sunbird** is the architect of a fairly large, untidy home, often created from a single type of material such as dry grass **(9)**. The nest of the **Scarlet-chested Sunbird** seen here has no porch **(10)**, even though the female was already incubating when this photograph was taken. The literature tells us that these sunbirds construct a porch, but this avant-garde pair obviously did not consult the relevant plans.

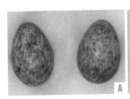

A Malachite
   Sunbird: 20mm
B Scarlet-chested
   Sunbird: 19mm

1

Holes in earth banks: The ground-borers

John Carlyon

2

3

Most **bee-eaters**, such as the **White-fronted (1)** and **Southern Carmine bee-eaters (2)**, excavate long tunnels in river banks, or in similar vertical or sloping earth structures, while others, notably the **Böhm's Bee-eater,** burrow into flat ground **(3)**, often in the proximity of rivers. A few species

4

are solitary, while others nest in large colonies.

A number of **kingfishers**, including **Pied (4)**, **Giant** and **Malachite kingfishers**, are also ground-borers – unlike their cousins, the so-called dryland kingfishers, which nest in natural tree holes.

A Southern Carmine Bee-eater: 26mm

B White-fronted Bee-eater: 22mm

C Giant Kingfisher: 45mm

D Pied Kingfisher: 29mm

Nests on water: Houseboats and mud cones

Several species construct nests that float on water. The **African Jacana (1)** builds a flimsy pad **(2)** consisting of plant stems overlaid on floating vegetation. The buoyant nests of the **Little Grebe (3)** and the **Great Crested Grebe (4)** are more substantial. Made of mounds of water plants, they are anchored to reeds or sedges to stop them drifting. Both species cover the eggs with

vegetation when leaving their nests. Another floating nester is the **Red-knobbed Coot (5)**. It constructs a large mound of aquatic vegetation **(6&7)** that is usually exposed on open water while anchored to reeds or sedges.

8

Lesser (8) and **Greater flamingos (9)** build conical nests made of mud, topped with a bowl-shaped hollow in which a single egg is laid. Using their beaks to push and smear the mud into shape, these colonial breeders construct nests of between 15 and 45cm in height – depending on how much mud is available in the vicinity. Occasionally flooding may wipe out the eggs of an entire colony. There are only a few permanent breeding locations in sub-Saharan Africa.

9

A Great Crested Grebe: 53mm
B Red-knobbed Coot: 54mm
C Greater Flamingo: 89mm
D Lesser Flamingo: 82mm

A

B

C

D

Excavated tree holes: The drilling brigade

John Carlyon

1

2

When it comes to home construction, **barbets** and **woodpeckers** are in a league of their own: they drill and chisel their own nest cavities in trees, the sole exception being the Ground Woodpecker, which digs a burrow in the ground. Barbets, like the **Black-collared Barbet (1)**, usually excavate their tunnels and nest chambers in

John Carlyon

3

dead or rotten tree trunks **(2)** or branches, preferring the underside of sloping branches. **Woodpeckers** such as the **Golden-tailed Woodpecker (3)** may excavate nest holes and cavities in either dead or living trees, although they favour the former. Other than accidentally furnishing their new homes with woodchips during excavation, these birds make no effort to line their nest chambers.

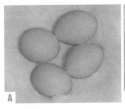

A

B

A Black-collared Barbet: 24mm
B Golden-tailed Woodpecker: 25mm

22

Why build a nest when there are so many natural tree holes available? Like many other species, **parrots**, **wood-hoopoes**, **rollers**, **oxpeckers**, **tits**, **hornbills** and **Glossy Starlings** make use of ready-made shelters. Most of these tree-hole breeders make no attempt to modify their temporary home, although the hornbills are an exception. When it is time for the female hornbill to lay her eggs, she encloses herself in her new residence by sealing the entrance with mud, and sometimes droppings, brought by the male, leaving only a narrow opening **(1)** through which to get food. The male will feed her for as long as she is immobile, as seen here by a male **Southern Yellow-billed Hornbill (2)**. Once the eggs have hatched and the young have started to fledge, the female breaks out, leaving her brood to reseal the entrance behind her. As they continue to grow, the chicks are fed by both parents. Unlike other hornbills, the **Southern Ground Hornbill (3)** does not seal the entrance to its large tree hole.

A **Southern Yellow-billed Hornbill: 37mm**
B **Southern Ground Hornbill: 74mm**

Robust tree nests: Bowls and platforms

The **Secretarybird (1)** constructs a large platform of sticks and other plant material at the top of a thorny bush or tree. Nests in continuous use can exceed a diameter of 2m and the pressure of their weight may push them to below the crown of the tree. The nest contains two, or occasionally three eggs. The central hollow is lined with grass – protective enough for chicks clamouring for food **(2)**; regurgitated pellets litter the nest rim and the ground below the tree. Seen from a distance, the white faecal sprays on a tree betray the location of a Secretarybird's nest.

The tree-nesting **White-backed** and **Lappet-faced vultures** build twig nests in the crowns of flat-topped trees, with the shallow central depression usually lined with dry grass. The nest of the White-backed Vulture **(3&4)** may reach 1m in diameter, and a single egg **(5a&b)**, 88 mm long, is laid. Very rarely are two eggs

produced. The Lappet-faced Vulture **(6)** constructs a huge nest **(7&8)**, which expands with regular use to more than 2m wide and 1m deep over a period of several years. Over time its weight will cause it to sink deeply into the crown. In areas where spotted

hyaenas and black-backed jackals are absent, regurgitated pellets usually accumulate under nesting trees, but where they are present, these predators frequently eat the pellets.

Martial **(9&10)** and **Crowned eagles (11)** create enormous structures that may measure, and even exceed, 2m in diameter. The nest of the Crowned Eagle can easily reach a depth of up to 3m. This bird of prey carries most of the construction material in its talons, but uses its beak to assemble the nest. Its nest is always placed in stout tree fork **(12)**, usually well above the ground, out of

Alan Weaving

Alan Weaving

reach of predators. Nests may be used year after year, with new nesting items added each breeding season. During the incubation and nestling period, fresh green leaves are regularly woven into the nest bowl. Usually 1–2 eggs are laid; where two eggs are produced only one chick is successfully raised.

Despite the size of its creator, the stick nest of the **Bateleur (13)** seldom exceeds 60cm in diameter and 30cm in depth. In the Bateleur nest seen here the large fledgling was within a few days of leaving the nest. This particular nest, located in Nairobi National Park, Kenya, had been in use for five years at the time this photograph was taken (1995).

Jackal Buzzards (14) normally build their bulky stick nests, some as wide as 70cm, on cliff ledges. However, in the open areas of the Karoo these birds nest in trees **(15)** and sometimes on the platforms of windmills. The nest bowl is lined with green leaves throughout the incubation and fledging periods **(16)**. A clutch of two eggs **(17)**, 60mm long, is produced. Rarely is one or even three eggs laid.

Cape (18) and Pied crows (19) also make their stick nests in trees, although they more commonly erect their homes on the top of telephone poles (20) – especially if trees are in short supply. They will also nest on windmill platforms and more rarely on rock ledges. The nest bowl is relatively deep and lined with wool, fur and feathers; in farming areas, nests may incorporate pieces of fencing wire and baling twine. Both species lay 4–5 eggs on average. Old crow nests (21) are commonly expropriated by raptors such as Lanner Falcons and Greater Kestrels for breeding.

A Crowned Eagle: 69mm
B Cape Crow: 45mm
C Pied Crow: 45mm

White-breasted Cormorants (22&23) are colonial breeders that nest in trees, on cliff ledges or more rarely on the ground.

Herons build large, untidy stick platforms lined with grass, usually in trees, with several pairs congregating in close proximity. The **Grey Heron's** grass-padded bowl **(24)** houses 2–4 eggs. The **Green-backed Heron (25)** constructs its twiggy nest on a low branch, well concealed in the foliage, close to or above the water. **Black-headed Heron** produce a clutch of 2–6 eggs **(26)**, in a saucer-shaped nest; the chicks **(27)** are fed by both parents.

28

29

30

The **Little Egret (28)** and the **Western Cattle Egret (29)** build tangled, saucer-shaped platforms **(30)** that are rarely more than 40cm in diameter. They breed in large mixed-species colonies in trees, often nesting side by side with other heron species, ibises and cormorants **(31)**. Little Egrets typically lay 2–3 eggs, which are 47mm long. Western Cattle Egrets produce 2–4 eggs.

A Grey Heron: 60mm
B Black-headed Heron: 62mm
C Western Cattle Egret: 45mm

31

A

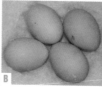

B

C

Unlike the ground-breeding **Great White Pelican**, the **Pink-backed Pelican** nests in trees, seen here with **African Sacred Ibises** and **Yellow-billed Storks (32)**.

Not easy to categorise, the massive communal nest **(33)** of the **Red-billed Buffalo Weaver (34)** is a rather robust twiggy affair, which is why we have listed it here under the tree nests. Several pairs may team up to construct a scruffy stick nest, with the males doing the heavy lifting and the females lining the nest chambers, of which there are usually two or more. Nest chambers are used for breeding and roosting. Most nests are built in trees, but they can also be found on telephone poles **(35)**, windmills **(36)** and cell masts. Egg clutches vary in colour and patterning; commonly only 3–4 eggs **(37a&b)**, 28mm long, are laid.

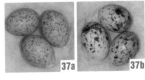

Flimsy stick nests: Ramshackle homes

Pigeons and **doves** take a somewhat less stylish approach to nest building. Seemingly casually flung together, the nests of these birds, including those of the **Cape Turtle (1&2)** and **Laughing (3&4) doves**, are an untidy tangle of twigs, grass stems and the occasional leaf in trees or bushes. So sparsely designed are the homes of these birds that, when viewed from below, one can sometimes see the eggs or nestlings through gaps in the nest floor. Strong winds are a threat, often resulting in the loss of a clutch or a brood.

1

2

3

John Carlyon

4

A **Cape Turtle Dove:** 28mm

B **Laughing Dove:** 26mm

A

B

Of all the doves and pigeons in the region, **Namaqua Doves (5)** build the flimsiest homes **(6)**. Their nests are seldom more than 1.5m above the ground, with some assembled on the ground and others on fallen branches, or sometimes on a grass tussock.

Speckled Pigeons (7) seek out secure locations such as rocky ledges or other solid surfaces to construct their nests. They also take advantage of man-made structures, which provide ample protection from both predators and the elements. The nest platform is usually constructed with whatever plant material is easiest to collect: twigs **(8)**, coarse grass or, in the case of one nest, pine needles **(9)**. In another case, a pair had chosen to nest in an old barn and the material closest to hand was baling twine and short sections of binding wire. The droppings of these pigeons are messy and relatively acidic.

African Penguins (1) nest in colonies, either on offshore islands or on the mainland, where they make their home in burrows, on the ground **(2)**, or against boulders or banks. Some nests may be lined with feathers and

dry plant materials. A clutch of two round white eggs **(3)**, 68mm in length, is the norm.

The **Cape Cormorant** nests in dense colonies **(4)**, usually on offshore islands. Its dwelling is a shallow bowl of sticks, seaweed and feathers on the ground **(5&6)**, in which 2–3 (sometimes up to 5) eggs **(7)** are laid. The eggs usually measure 55mm in length.

The nest of the **Crowned Cormorant (8)** is similar to that of the Cape Cormorant and may incorporate seaweed, feathers, bones and pieces of plastic, an all too common feature of coastal nests. Normally 2–4 pale blue to chalky-coloured eggs are produced.

A nesting colony of **Cape Gannets (9)** is the avian equivalent of the microflats that characterise high-density cities such as Hong Kong. Despite hundreds of nests abutting each other in a vast colony, the gannet pair are able to locate their home when returning from the fishing grounds. Each nest is a shallow saucer-like depression in a mound of seaweed, guano and feathers. A single egg **(10)**, 82mm long, is usually laid.

As with other gulls, the nest of the **Kelp Gull (11)** is a shallow scrape sparsely lined with seaweed, grass, sticks and feathers. **Hartlaub's Gulls (12)** create shallow bowl-like nests fitted with grass, twigs, feathers and other debris, such as mussel shells. Kelp Gulls produce 1–3 eggs **(13)**, while Hartlaub's Gulls lay two eggs **(14)**.

Although they usually nest on the ground, **Egyptian Geese (15)** favour a variety of sites, from cliff ledges, large tree forks and deserted buildings **(16)** to the crowns of Hamerkop nests and abandoned crow and raptor nests. The nest hollow is lined with the belly down of the female, which she uses to cover the eggs when absent. Egg teeth **(17&18)**, visible at the beak tip of the hatchlings, are used to crack open the egg from the inside. Once hatched, the goslings **(19)** plunge to the ground in a leap of faith as the female calls to them from terra firma.

The **Southern Pochard (20)** creates a relatively deep bowl lined with vegetation and sometimes female belly down. Usually well hidden among grass or reeds, the nests **(21)** are quite similar in structure to those of other ducks.

1

Bare ground nests: The Spartans

The world's largest living bird, the **Common Ostrich (1)** makes its nest on the bare ground or in a superficial scrape. In addition to the main hen, several other females may lay their eggs in the same nest, where up to 21 eggs may accumulate. These eggs **(2)** are the largest laid by any bird, each weighing up to 1.5kg. A single Common Ostrich egg is roughly equivalent to 24 domestic hen eggs **(3)**, and its average length is 148mm. Males take an active role in incubation, working the night shift while females take their turn during the day. The creamy white colour of the Common Ostrich's eggs is unusual among those of ground-nesting birds; in most other species the eggs have camouflage colours and markings. The bird's large size and aggressive nature provide the necessary armoury to keep predators away from its eggs and hatchlings **(4)**.

2

3

4

A coastal wader, the **African (Black) Oystercatcher (5)** excavates a shallow scrape in the sand along the coast, but makes no attempt to embellish it with extra material. The female lays two strongly marked eggs **(6)**. As these birds breed during the peak holiday season, they are at risk of being disturbed by dogs and human traffic along the coastline.

Pied Avocets incubate their eggs in nests on the open ground or, in the case of the bird shown here, along the edge of a coastal sand dune **(7)**. A depression, formed by a donkey's hoof print, makes for a perfect, although unadorned, nest **(8)**.

The long-legged **Black-winged Stilt** lays its 3–4 eggs **(9)** in a shallow hollow, which it fills with a few small sticks and other debris. Some individuals construct more substantial nests of plant material.

Most **plovers** and other **waders** use no nest material although some, such as this **Three-banded Plover (10)**, scrape together a few flat pebbles to form a base on which the female can lay her eggs. The small White-fronted Plover, mainly a coastal species, decorates its egg base with small pieces of mollusc shell.

All **lapwings**, including the **Crowned**, **Wattled** and **Blacksmith lapwings**, lay their cryptically marked eggs in shallow ground scrapes, usually in open, exposed sites. The nests are lined with bits of vegetation, dry mud and ungulate dung pellets that provide

good camouflage for the eggs, making it difficult to locate them. Both the male and female of all lapwing species will dive-bomb and attack intruders, including errant elephants and buffaloes.

The **Crowned Lapwing (11)** is amazingly trusting of humans and often nests on lawns in suburban and even urban environments, as well as on grass verges along busy roads. A clutch of 2–4 eggs **(12)** is laid. Mortality in urban areas is quite high, with the domestic cat being a prolific killer of these birds. The **Wattled Lapwing (13)** prefers to nest in short grassland, often just after a fire when the first green starts to show. The clutch usually consists of four eggs **(14)**. The densely patterned eggs **(15)** of the **Blacksmith Lapwing** are 40mm long.

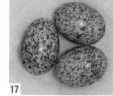

As with all other **sandgrouse** species, the **Namaqua Sandgrouse (16)** deposits three eggs **(17)**, 36mm in length, in a shallow scrape **(18)** sparsely decorated with a few stones and plant fragments.

Like most **coursers**, **Temminck's Courser (19)** produces 1–2 eggs **(20)** on bare ground – although some of its cousins ring their nests with, or make a partial bed of, antelope droppings to help camouflage the eggs. Unlike its relatives, the **Three-banded Courser** usually partially buries its eggs in soft soil.

All **terns**, including the **Swift Tern (21)**, lay their eggs on sand or gravel **(22)**, and make no attempt to create scrapes or to adorn their homes with nesting items. One egg **(23)** is usually laid, which is 62mm in length.

A Spotted Thick-knee: 52mm
B Water Thick-knee: 50mm

The **Spotted Thick-knee (24)**, or Dikkop, lays its eggs directly on the ground where the eggs **(25)** and chicks **(26)** are difficult to spot. This species has managed to survive and breed in suburban areas, relying on camouflage to avoid detection. Unfortunately, some are taken by domestic cats and dogs.

Nightjars, such as the **Rufous-cheeked Nightjar (27)**, produce 1–2 eggs **(28)** on bare ground, on rocks or in leaf litter; no attempt is made to make a scrape or add nesting material. The birds as well as their eggs are camouflaged for protection.